10192

HOW TO CREATE YOUR OWN
DYNAMIC MISSION STATEMENT
THAT WORKS

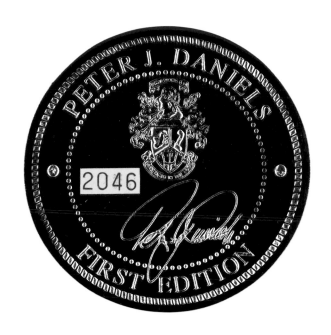

PETER J. DANIELS

2046

FIRST EDITION

HOW TO CREATE YOUR OWN DYNAMIC

MISSION STATEMENT

THAT WORKS

A MANUAL FOR A COMMITTED LIFE

PETER J DANIELS

Other Titles by Peter J. Daniels:
How To Be Happy Though Rich
How to Reach Your Life Goals
How To Handle A Major Crisis
How To Be Motivated All The Time
How To Have The Awesome Power of Public Speaking
Miss Phillips You Were Wrong!
Global Summary Into Multi-Level Marketing

Tutorial programs:
Destiny
How To Get More Done And Have Time Left Over

All correspondence to:
World Centre for Entrepreneurial Studies
38-40 Carrington Street, Adelaide, South Australia 5000
Telephone: (08) 231 0111   Facsimile: (08) 211 8423

Published by

World Centre for Entrepreneurial Studies
38-40 Carrington Street, Adelaide, South Australia 5000
Telephone: 61-8-231 0111   Facsimile: 61-8-211 8423

Dedicated to

Dr Harrold Steward,
who has spent a lifetime
influencing the mission of others.

Contents

CONTENTS

Preface

PREFACE

This book can be for you a blueprint for success and priority living that will clarify your direction and make the journey of life more enjoyable. The following pages will guide you into a "take charge" lifestyle that puts you at the control levers of your life. For some this may become unsettling, because there is within that unforgiving framework a "no let out" clause for personal and corporate accountability.

As you first create and then pursue your *dynamic mission statement that works*, you will experience a new and exciting sense of fulfilment that will permit you to look with greater confidence towards a more productive future, with the means of transportation to the realisation of your productive dreams clearly defined.

Why Have A Mission Statement At All?

A mission statement can be described as a written statement of purpose and behavioural boundaries worthy of a life's pursuit.

CHAPTER ONE

Why Have A Mission Statement At All?

I have been involved in business for over 35 years, coming into contact with people from all walks of life in many countries of the world. I have observed that most serious, thinking people have a mission statement of some kind. For others it seems to be a matter of survival. They drift through life with a hope that some external force or circumstances will make life better, easier and more fulfilling, only to arrive at middle life or old age full of excuses, disappointments, frustrations and bitterness; often they blame others and expect someone miraculously to recognise the true value of their existence, even though their personal contribution was only survival. Lack of direction limits their response to a growing world, with expanding needs and opportunities.

But what if you just want to be left alone, to do your own thing in your own way? Is it still helpful to have a mission statement? The answer is a resounding yes!! It will provide an even more balanced and fulfilling way of doing just what you want — because you have within your grasp an opportunity called *life* and you will always want both to protect yourself against threats and to take advantage of challenges, which indicates the real value you place upon it.

A mission statement can also stimulate you to think and assess yourself against what opportunities are available. It gives security and a standard against which a changing world and personal circumstances can be measured. This will often provide some clear guidelines that have been carefully thought out when there was time for reflection and assessment. A mission statement also allows you in difficult times and crises to fall back on the realities of who you are and what you stand for in respect to your responsibilities and obligations, as well as for your own preservation.

A mission statement is particularly helpful if you are in a small business, and essential if you run a large corporation or organisation. As a matter of fact, I am involved in some situations around the world where the mission statement is read aloud at board meetings to remind all those present of the clear boundaries of operation. This is particularly helpful because it tends to remove fuzzy thinking and prevents discussion and decisions from getting off the track.

A personal or corporate mission statement can even work in conjunction with someone else's mission statement. You may want to work with a partner but still want to specify your own mission within theirs.

It would be helpful at this point to submit some definitions to prevent confusion in respect to other areas of personal and corporate management.

Mission Statement:

Definitions:
- A mission statement sets a pattern of behaviour that exhibits the character of an organisation or person.

- A mission statement is a style of pursuit.

- A mission statement provides the ethos for an organisation or person.

- A mission statement reflects the spirit rather than the law of a person or organisation.

- A mission statement creates the relationship culture of a person or organisation.

- A mission statement is a quasi trustee of a person or organisation.

- A mission statement is a secure anchor in the stormy seas of life.

A mission statement can be described as a written statement of purpose and behavioural boundaries worthy of a life's pursuit.

Notes

In other words, it reveals to the world the depth or otherwise of your personal commitment and ethics which provides stability for your life. A mission statement usually describes a particular type of journey involving a moral stand predicated upon a strong commitment to a belief.

When an individual or a group is committed to "a mission", then the matter at hand takes on a singular passion because it is energised by the morality factor that will provide the inner strength to finish what was started.

Very often in a "mission situation" the final goal or objectives become secondary and the journey pre-eminent. That is why you will often hear very successful people say that the journey was more exhilarating than the destination. Sticking to a plan requires a sense of mission and without it, many good intentions are never brought to fruition. We often spend all our time, thought and effort focusing on the final destination, without taking into consideration the quality of the journey.

Only despots justify questionable means to reach their end.

In coming to grips with personal or corporate mission statements, the means to the end is often of paramount importance because it shows continually the quality and intensity of the mission.

The style of a mission always determines the type and quality of people that will readily join you, and the way they will carry out their task, which provides an automatic filtering system giving some guarantee of the types of people suitable for the task ahead.

A correct and explicit mission statement prevents misunderstanding and declares at the outset the means of transportation. By its very charter, it will exclude or include those who can live comfortably within its boundaries. It will also help to identify those who could initially seem suitable but during the process prove unsatisfactory.

Ignoring or manipulating a mission statement will surely cause disruption to those who are trying to work within the company code. Such an attitude develops insecurity, distrust and a definite slowing down of the mission. For individuals to try and adjust their mission statement to suit a particular set of circumstance can only mean that . . .

1. the mission statement was not thoroughly thought out in the first place, or that . . .

2. your value system has changed, or . . .

3. the destination is still not clear.

A mission statement that is ambiguous, sloppy and open to manipulation always provides a way for the unscrupulous to enter and the uncommitted to exit.

Beware of long explanations and justifications in respect to the changing, manipulating or overriding of a mission statement.

During times of stress, changing markets and new personnel, keep in mind that the mission statement

Notes

was carefully thought out, and included an assessment of the future. It is the ethical guide for all who have accepted to work within its charter.

There is a strange phenomenon that always seems to blow the cover of power holders. They use threats and logic to gain control, or change the text or the meaning of an agreed mission statement to make it fit into a personal agenda. Before hiring or creating a working relationship with anyone, ask them for a personal assessment of the mission statement and then measure their agreement against its charter.

A mission statement is also a moral check on unbridled ambitions.

It is often too late in the middle of a quest to evaluate the ethics of an enterprise or a relationship. That is why the desire to achieve and enjoy the fruits of power and wealth should always carry with it the responsibility of agreed direction and moral behaviour.

Entrepreneurs can never be stereotyped because they come in all types. They can be gregarious, bullies, methodical, sloppy, generous or greedy; but almost without exception, they have twelve indispensable qualities that set them apart from everyone else.

1. They have drive and will keep going when everyone else has given up and gone home.

2. They are persuasive in their quest to get others to see and follow through with their point of view.

3. They have perception and can see what is not distinguishable to others, and believe what others find unbelievable.

4. They have strong ego needs that compel them to win, sometimes at any cost.

5. They can respond to failure and crises with optimism.

6. They have confidence in their own ability to adjust and win in changing circumstances.

7. They know what their inner beliefs will permit them to do.

8. They plan strategies and measure their progress continually.

9. They have a short term view when assessing performance and a long term view when assessing success.

10. Their final destination has clear, measurable and specific time, quality and quantitative values.

Notes

11. They are mentally accurate and objectively urgent in all their deliberations.

12. They tend to choose people to assist them with strengths that they do not have, to fill in the gaps.

These twelve qualities are very powerful and that is why there is a need for them to be kept in check by a moral code which can be expressed through a mission statement. To stage a full frontal attack on a person with a strong ego is inviting trouble, and the clarity of direction is often lost in the argument of justification. It can be very difficult to bring an ambitious person from the brink of unbecoming conduct by using moral logical argument, but a mission statement can be very effective because it points out clearly the real basis of agreed responsibility.

Always remind yourself and others of the mission statement and refer to it regularly for assessment before, during and after decisions.

Goals:
Definition: A goal is a predetermined achievement in life — it is a destination, not a journey — in contrast to a mission statement which declares the all encompassing means to that end.

A goal is a specific desire for a predetermined future event shaped into a step-by-step plan which includes a time frame, contingency plans and measurements.

Objectives:
Definition: Objectives are intermediary steps through life and act as stepping stones between destinations.

They are building blocks to all goals.

Objectives are always subject to the mission statement, which provides the conduct and passion needed to energise the commitment.

Affirmation:
Definition: An affirmation is very often printed on a card that can be carried with you, to be read and used to affirm your commitment. This will increase your determination to get the job done.

An affirmation card is particularly helpful as a reminder of your specific goals. It will sharpen your focus and stimulate an acceleration to perform.

Some people make a list, first declaring the long term goals, followed by the intermediary objectives and then the mission statement, concluding with an affirmation.

All of these units are helpful towards achieving success in whatever you have chosen as your life's contribution, but for this book, I want to examine, explain and provide some mission statement tools that have thus far been overlooked in detailed form in business education and literature.

Notes

CHAPTER TWO

The Benefits of Having a Mission Statement

A mission statement reveals in very clear terms your person and personality. It will expand and limit your involvement in areas relative to your self-discovery.

CHAPTER TWO

The Benefits of Having a Mission Statement

Who are you?

Most people go through life without making the most exciting journey that is available to all mankind — the journey of self-discovery. Why not take a day or a week out of your life to spend on your most important unexplored asset — yourself! After careful thought write down what your first choice would be regarding the style and quality of the personality you would like to have. Give some thought about the kind of friends that you would like to make, and the quality of character you could admire in yourself. A difficult task? Of course it is — but all this and many other tasks will be easier, and will even be self-revealing, when you discover how to create your own *dynamic mission statement that works.* A well thought out mission statement will reveal quite clearly who you are. It will determine what you will read and study, and who you will make friends with. It will also determine your economics, clarify and test your religious and political convictions, and determine your business path, family and social relationships.

In other words a mission statement reveals in very clear terms your person and personality. It will expand and limit your involvement in areas relative to your self-discovery.

Wouldn't it be a great pity to arrive at a time in life when you could look back and see large portions of life's opportunities missed because you had not discovered one of the most important people in the universe — *yourself.*

Do not be discouraged if on first sight of what you believe to be your true self you see only limitations and contradictions. Persevere! Avoid the "WHAT IFS" — such as *WHAT IF* I were another person, then I could do extraordinary things. *WHAT IF* I were built differently and could be more attractive. *WHAT IF* the circumstances that I now live under were different, and *WHAT IF* I were younger, with more time.

Rather, use "BECAUSE" — *BECAUSE* I am now looking into my life I will discover new talents. *BECAUSE* I am built in a special way I have advantages. *BECAUSE* I live in this time in history I am blessed with opportunity, and *BECAUSE* I am older, I have seasoning.

My good friends, Dr Robert Schuller, W.Clement Stone and the late Dr Norman Vincent Peale, have built a lifetime of involvement touching the four corners of the earth, encouraging others to think positively, and to look into themselves with the help of God to discover their own dynamic uniqueness.

Your mission statement will help you to discover, declare and determine your future.

(We deal with this in more detail in respect to your *dynamic mission statement that works* in Chapter 4 under "describe yourself".)

Security

One of the great tragedies of the human race is the insecurity and lack of confidence that is felt by many people, and even those who have a facade of superiority.

Wealth, poverty, fame and even knowledge can often give a sense of security, but when the difficulties come and positioning fades, then confidence and security seem all too often to fade with it. Those who wanted and have fought for wealth, power and fame, have sometimes sought it as a antidote for insecurity, only to find that after the glow of receiving, the uncertainty often remains; and those who accepted the mantle of poverty as a badge of honour also eventually realise its powerlessness.

A dynamic mission statement will give a large degree of security by providing a benchmark for all that would threaten to jeopardise the normal pillars of confidence, namely decisiveness, simplicity and direction.

Notes

Decisiveness

One of the most difficult tasks humans have to wrestle with is decision making. So often we delay so long, on the pretext of needing more information, that the decision is made by events overtaking us. But the possession of a mission statement will provide strong, clear boundaries within which decisions become speedier, easier and better.

Let me give a simple example. The telephone rings and the caller would like you to get involved in some worthy project that they feel passionately about. They are quite sure that you should become involved as well. Rather than get into debate and discussion, which would take time and energy, and cause anxiety, you examine your mission statement and realise the project is not in the direction of your life's agenda. So you are able to respond either by telling the caller that it is not in the direction you are going and you need to politely decline, or, if it is in the direction that you are travelling, then you can accept immediately. A mission statement will provide this much needed assurance.

There is great security in being competently decisive and at the same time knowing that you have made the right decision. It will also preserve your mental energy.

Simplicity

Security is always found in simplicity and understanding. The more parts there are to a machine, the more chance there is of a breakdown. So it is with life. Your life can maintain a simplicity through a comprehensive and concise mission statement because it keeps life uncomplicated.

Frustrations often come from lack of clear thinking.

I have found that simple, clear guidelines with character are always reflected in clear thinking. A thinking process without the baggage of complications is usually predicated upon truth, and the Bible says that *the truth will set you free.* That also means freedom from insecurity.

Simplicity, I might add, does not mean loose ends, lack of imagination or abandonment of order, but rather, it means exactly the opposite. Simplicity demands order!

A dynamic mission statement that works will assist you in the quest for true simplicity which has its own style, in thought, word and deed, and can be exhibited at any economic or social level of life. That is one of the true marks of a genius.

Direction

It is an inexplicable fact that a mission statement will give direction because the very basis of a mission statement is directional. What is not usually recognised is that a mission statement, when properly used, can be a basis for creative thinking, stimulates the mind to be more focused and prevents wandering and displacements of concentration.

Imagine the security you could obtain through your mission statement by directional thought, energy and decisions, all made in harmony with each other. The

Notes

achievement thrust would be enormous and the energy saved would provide more time to explore and utilise your unlimited possibilities.

Consider the opposite if you will. A goal or a destination without any directions to lead the way and keep you on course will quickly lead to prevailing indecision. Yes, a dynamic mission statement is the compass of life setting the directions towards your goals. You need it just as surely as a train needs tracks to run on. With your dynamic mission statement you will have the conditions, guidance and balance that make high speed travel much safer.

Many great leaders and entrepreneurs have fallen by the wayside because they lost direction in their means of transportation toward their dreams. A dynamic mission statement will provide that direction. As a matter of fact, it has often been said that successful people make decisions quickly and change them rarely, and unsuccessful people make decisions slowly and change them often. I would suggest that a mission statement can provide that kind of confidence.

Fulfilment

One of the great character traits of any achiever, in any field, is energy. I never cease to be amazed at the vibrant energy of successful people, even into what some would consider old age. I have often observed a man or woman, half the age of a senior achiever, huffing and puffing trying to keep up or falling asleep; the older person is moving into second gear while the younger one is ready to accept that all doors of opportunity are closed regarding a particular event, only to find the senior citizen is seeking and finding and progressing towards further attainment.

A mission statement, properly prepared, is an energy sustainer and a daily assessment to be reckoned with. There is even some evidence to suggest that a profound mission statement, carefully prepared and executed, will extend a life span because of its recuperative powers.

Remember, of course, that the mission statement belongs to you. In a real sense it is your own measured working personality, which means that you can face life boldly, accepting its harsh scrutiny on terms that *you* have carefully considered, rather than accepting circumstances that are thrust upon you as your inevitable unchartered lot in life.

Your dynamic mission statement is, in effect, a trade-off against life and will channel your ambition in measurable stages, giving you a fulfilled life that has substance and satisfaction. A fulfilling life is an abundant life and should be a grateful response to our Creator, acknowledging the opportunity given with serious, thoughtful and thorough attention towards its implementation.

Notes

Break the Confusion Trap

Remember that you or your organisation must give life to the mission through the dynamics of vision, commitment and energy, which provide the fuel that will give it life.

CHAPTER THREE

Break the Confusion Trap

I trust by now we have removed some of the confusion surrounding the mystery of a mission statement. Before we embark on the process, it would be good to reinforce some of the do's and don'ts of *creating your own dynamic mission statement that works*.

The operative words here are *your, mission,* and *works*.

For anything to work you must have an owner to energise and create the continued thrust to get things done. To make your mission work requires qualities such as wisdom, knowledge and timing which are indispensable to all achievement. The mission statement of an organisation or an individual has its own entity and takes on its own characteristics, with all the ramifications of a personality.

Without you or your company's input, a mission statement is a lifeless piece of paper. It may be inter-

esting to read, but it is without the lifegiving breath
that can only come from involved humanity.
Remember that you or your organisation must give life
to the mission through the dynamics of vision,
commitment and energy, which provide the fuel that
will give it life. The bottom line is simply this —
*mission statements cannot work without the input of
human commitment*; so be sure you are prepared to
activate a mission statement by examining yourself to
find the real reason you would like to have one, rather
than just feeling that you should.

The power of a mission statement and its importance is revealed to the extent that it represents the life
of a person or a corporation; it then commands the
total support which legitimises its workings. Whatever
happens, don't be overawed by the size of your goal or
of your mission statement. Start out with an exper-
imental one and test its authenticity and reality in your
day by day living. Avoid adjusting it to suit circumstances, but rather fine-tune it by the standards you set
for yourself or your organisation, so creating and
establishing a special ethos and a code of behaviour
that can be kept and nurtured in secret as well as being
a commanding and respectful public document.

Realise that confusion usually burns up more energy
and destroys more lives than bad decisions. The fact is
that you *can* correct something but you *cannot* correct
nothing. So keep your mission statement simple,
measurable, direct and clear.

Ignoring your mission statement once it has been
prepared, and allowing the circumstances of life to
overpower you, will destroy your power of choice and
confirm the dictum ... Confusion always paralyses
progress.

Time and thought spent wrestling with the mission statement and getting it right will save light years of uncertainty and wasted energy; so be prepared to give the mission statement the respect it requires.

Always be careful that the circumstances of life do not lead you away from your mission statement into the melting pot of chance, allowing someone or events to reset your reactions and in the process rob you of the realisation that every human being is a child of God and designed for achievement.

Do not be tempted into doing what is expected of you but examine and provoke your own expectations by resisting the temptations of peer pressure and the direction of the crowd.

Here are a few simple questions to ask yourself or the organisation you represent. They will clarify motives, motions and morality.

1. Do you know what you want to achieve?

Knowing exactly what you want to achieve is 75% of its fulfilment. To some this hardly seems an accurate statement, but I will stand by it.

Past experience demonstrates to me that all else seems to fall into place once that decision is made. Ideas and possibilities begin to form when you know what you really want to do. Unfortunately the *idea* of a

---

Notes

fulfilling goal is nothing more than just an idea; it lacks the commitment and the sustaining passion of a life-time pledge. Ask yourself these questions in respect to what you want to achieve: Is it believable to you? Is it a fad or a fact? Is it only fashionable for now? Or is it a decision based on emotion and feelings rather than an investigative search that has been brooded on and wrestled with to finally stand without doubt as a light in the darkness? Any thought of achievement must carry with it the acceptance of responsibility towards fulfilment, and this must not be predicated on the guaranteed performance of others.

These few short paragraphs of soul-searching questions represent the foundation towards that which activates *a dynamic mission statement that works*, and it is from the depths and power of this decision that all else will stand. The question, *Do you know what you want to achieve?* can easily be answered by grandiose schemes and fantasy thinking, but I am asking you to respond to the question in the context of raw reality. If you play the fool here, then your blunder will reveal itself at a time much later in your life with energies and time wasted and opportunities lost.

Answer the question, *Do you know what you want to achieve?* Write it down and then go on to the next question with confidence.

Here are some suggested thought stimulators to get you going:

(1) The fact that you are reading this book is a strong indication that you have something inside trying desperately to get out.

(2) Why not look at your life thus far and consider what you could have accomplished if you had given it more careful thought?

(3) Do you envy someone who has achieved a great deal in a particular area of life?

(4) When you read an adventure novel or a biography, do you read yourself into the leading role?

(5) Consider spending a day alone in a library or park and contemplate what the future could hold for you.

(6) Why not make it a matter of prayer?

(7) Meet with six friends and have a dream session together. Have the people tell you what they think you could do to be great, and then do the same for them.

(8) Do you consider circumstances, background or other people as restraints on your life? If so you are overlooking the fact that many other people worse off than you have achieved great things.

Notes

(9) If you could accept the premise that nothing is impossible for you, what would be the most realistic future for you?

If you are still stuck, then maybe you need to read at least ten exciting biographies of major achievers.

2. Can you give an "impacts reason why"?

Now we find out whether or not the emotions were more in control than reason.

It is very easy to make a quick and passionate decision by emotion, but far more time consuming and difficult to make a reasoned decision. When reason and passion come together with the added ingredient of measured commitment, then the mix becomes very powerful indeed.

To give an "impacts reason why" is in a sense what the French call the *raison d'etre* (the reason for being), and to have an achievement goal without a specific impact may only mean that the motive is self indulgence. If that *is* correct, what is the measurable impact on your inner feelings? And will your feelings always be the same? And how reliable for tangible long term results are your emotional returns? Carefully assess your motives, because if they are not strong and clear, your energy and commitment may not stand the test of time. The present need to impress yourself or others will lose its attraction as the climb becomes more difficult.

Remember that many ego needs fade with time and fashion, and the "impacts reason why", if answered under the bright light of insight and truth, will add enormous power and drive to your quest, provide accurate information for your mission statement, and give a great boost to your confidence.

Here are some questions that will help you to come to an "impacts reason why."

Why will it impact?
How will it impact?
Where will it impact?
When will it impact?
How long will the impact last?
Will the impact totally satisfy me?

When answering these and other questions in this book, avoid generalities or answers that would necessarily sound clever or even reasonable if someone else were by chance to come across your notes. The crucial point here is that it must be for you and you alone. You must be satisfied with the answer, and if you are creating an answer that only reflects your public or perceived public image, then you have completely missed the point.

So often the real answer to the questions in respect to the perceived impact of your mission is lost in the description of the destination; there is no measurement which demands a specific result which will show up the inaccuracies.

Without an impact statement, you are like someone playing football without keeping the score, and to keep

Notes

the score you need to have some way of measuring victory. Many years can be wasted by working or studying carelessly towards an achievement that has not been subjected to a real time and impact study.

3. Are there any limiting factors?

So often we look at a possibility and see what we believe to be unscalable walls and blockages that seem impossible to overcome, only to find that some time later someone else has bridged the gap and got the job well and truly done. Beware! Those things you consider to be limiting factors may only be limits you have imposed upon yourself rather than having them imposed by other genuine external factors.

There are, of course, many real limiting factors, such as laws, physical and mental capacities and those of positioning. The key is to remember that most things change any number of times over a long lifetime. The lack of opportunity today may present itself rather surprisingly as a new or different opportunity tomorrow. Look circumspectly at real obstacles that cannot be moved and seek substitutes, or circumnavigate the obstacle and allow it to remain — maybe in time it, too, will become obsolete.

Clearly identify the unknowns in writing and treat them as loose cannons on a ship at sea until you can pin them down with clarification. Limiting factors are sometimes submerged like an iceberg and often only present themselves when they are confronted by progress. You may find that their construction may have deep foundations that have stood the test of time and have been unsuccessfully challenged by others. Do not waste your life by confronting an obstacle that cannot be moved, because of material substance, or the inertia of other people or events that could rob you of your life's blood and present you with nothing but frustration and inevitable failure.

When embarking on any venture that requires innovation and co-operation, assume the role of the devil's advocate and seek out ways in which you could, if you wanted to, stop the project. Then accept the possibility that others may be able to stop it that way too. Looking at the limiting factors in relationship to your mission statement prevents a pseudo rationale that could lull you into a false sense of security, only to have your dreams and aspirations crushed by a turn of events that was not considered.

By investigating the limiting factors, you are protecting yourself and preparing yourself to handle successfully any variation in the events of life and also giving some guarantee to the fulfilment of *your dynamic mission statement that works.*

4. **What personal and material tools do you need to get the job done?**

During the most desperate days of World War II, when England was faced with the possibility of defeat

---

Notes

by Adolf Hitler, the spirit of the British Empire was
kept alive by the words and wisdom of Sir Winston
Churchill. England was producing war material at an
accelerated pace, but even then they could not keep up
with what was required. The United States of America
was concerned about the possible effects if Adolf
Hitler were successful, as was the rest of the world, and
yet they were reluctant to get involved at that stage.
Understanding, but not agreeing, with the reluctant
position taken by the United States of America, Sir
Winston Churchill appealed to them for war
machinery in words that today remain as famous as
when he sent them this message: "Give us the tools and
we will finish the job". Of course, the United States
responded and finally became directly involved
themselves.

To do your life's work will also require many tools,
and to attempt to do the job without them is not wise,
as it will cause difficulty and even defeat. Examine
with some deliberation the exact tools that you will
require in the following areas.

Education

Are there some areas of education that you need to
undertake to be able to come to grips with the obstacles
to accomplishing what is required? Or, alternatively,
are you able to buy the services of someone else who
will fill the gap for you? Be very careful here not to take
the easy way out and put yourself under the supposed
educated opinion of someone else and become domi-
nated, misguided or bogged down by theory rather
than reality.

Skills

There are some skills that are essential for success that can only be acquired by experience and sensitivity. The way you treat other people, your style of dress, your conversation and voice standard in various situations can be learned by putting yourself deliberately in exceptional company, even if you have to get into that level of society by becoming a food or drink waiter at a high-class restaurant. Your skill in being with and handling other people is one of the most valuable assets you can have and should be continually developed. The famous J.D. Rockefeller once supposedly said, "I will pay more for the person with the ability to handle people than any other purchasable commodity under Heaven!" The value of getting along on a personal level with other people must never be minimised.

Positioning

It is of no advantage to develop the education and skills you need to achieve in a particular direction if you are far removed from the place of action. I am not referring to geography but rather being at or near the cross-roads of the activity of your choice. In this modern world with rapid transport and communi-

---

Notes

cation facilities, it is quite possible in many areas of involvement to conduct a great deal of enterprise without any personal interaction. But beware that personal interaction is not replaced by paper or other communication methods which do not have the impact and dynamics of personal representation and people skills that often produces the extra edge needed to get the job done.

Influence

Many years ago a great man called Dale Carnegie said in one of his books, "If you want to gather honey, don't kick over the bee hive". I received the same advice some time ago from a wise businessman when he counselled me in a situation with a very difficult person. He said, "Don't close the door". The people you do not need or want today may well be needed and wanted tomorrow, so guard your personal influence as a very powerful medium which cannot be purchased at any price. It carries with it the added power of attraction called sincerity. I always try to help as many people as I can in my journey through life, and if I am ever forced to close the door on a relationship, then I close it quietly and with good manners because I may find in the future I need to open it again when I need help.

Money

I wrote a book called *How To Be Happy Though Rich* many years ago. The cover showed me sitting on the hood of my gold Rolls Royce. One day I was approached by a middle-aged lady who recognised me in a hotel corridor. She said quite emphatically to me, "I'm not interested in money". My immediate response took her somewhat by surprise; I held out my hand and said, "Then give it to me". The woman was nonplussed and then said quickly, "I didn't mean it like that," and then we both laughed. As you move through the corridors of life, it will soon become very apparent that at every level of endeavour money requires no interpretation and is understood by all. Endeavour always to keep your own personal finances in order and build a sound reputation for stability in this area.

Money is almost always available for sound ventures. This is especially true when the seeker of that money has a sound proven track record for fiscal responsibility. To earn or acquire access to money requires a recipient's respect and understanding of its elusive nature.

5. Do you see any possible exit points?

When confronted by a major plan or a life goal, the possibility of having exit points is rarely contemplated because it smacks of surrendering or giving up. In my book *How to Reach Your Life Goals*, I suggest that we should look at expandable goals, because in ten or twenty years time we are entirely different people. Our

Notes

earlier needs and wants will have been dispensed with, and the world will be a very different place in which to live. How sad it is to meet someone who has achieved all they want to achieve in life and has become listless and lifeless. It reminds me of an ancient historical military figure who wept because there were no more worlds to conquer.

Consider the possibility of exit points in the time frame of your mission in case —

(a) the job is done by someone else

(b) the original goal is no longer valid or

(c) your needs and desires can no longer be met by these means.

The other possibility, of course, is that your goal does have a finality quotient and therefore your mission has a maximum time frame, which suggests another two possibilities:

(1) You can use the flexibility of your mission to adapt to other challenges, and the distance that you have travelled could be used as a stepping stone towards a different or larger target.

(2) Often (particularly if you are in your mid-thirties or under) the distance that you can see into the future is predicated upon the past and the excitement of the present conditioning of what you believe to be your ultimate quest at

that age. This tends to be readjusted as events change. Unless you are absolutely committed to a goal for life, and mean it, then exit points or variations may be of little interest to you.

To continue against provable, overwhelming, senseless odds can leave you weary, broken and bitter. It's much wiser to accept the change of circumstances and opportunities as a challenge to adapt, which if done practically and positively can produce new energy. In some cases it can take more courage and wisdom to *stop* than to continue. An exit point may also come as a gift, allowing you to stand back and reflect upon what has happened from a renewed perspective and open up a Pandora's box of exciting possibilities. Always remember that your future can be your friend if you welcome it and work towards it with positive expectancy.

6. How big do you want it to be in measurable terms?

This is another one of the difficult questions you will be asked in this book. My business experience and participation in seminars around the world has proven to me that the size of a life's impact is often left to chance and adjusted as time and opportunity grow or fade. To come to such an enormous decision will

---

Notes

create considerable pain. Declaring how big you want your goal to be will demand that you set in place a *dynamic mission statement that must work*, with a deep assessment made that reflects the size of the demand you have placed upon your life. Coming to grips with an assessment of size will provide a touch of reality. If approached honestly, it presupposes some personal realities that have been thoroughly investigated. How can we come to grips with what we need for a journey if we do not know the distance of the journey and its implications! I am sure that as you are going through each of the processes outlined in this book so far, the possibility of creating your own mission statement that works has taken on a new meaning, with more implications and more serious reckoning than you earlier anticipated. Yet if you ponder the question for another moment, you will very quickly come to the conclusion that the difficulty in stipulating a qualified size for a goal indicates there is some confusion surrounding the goal.

We commonly use ambiguous phrases such as "as big as I can", "as much as needed", "enough to make me happy" or "billions" and so on. This illustrates our inability or unwillingness to come to grips with the question, and tends to create invisible or vague targets that become difficult to hit. Getting people to declare a well thought-out measurement towards a predetermined goal is one of the most frustrating and difficult tasks I have in assisting people to achieve their dreams.

One of the great privileges in my life is that I have worked with some of the greatest corporate giants and thinkers of this century. I have often asked them this loaded question: "Do you have any regrets?" Almost without exception they respond, "If I knew I was going to achieve this much, I would have set my sights much higher". So the final question in this portion of this book is, "Are you thinking big enough?" If you are still in a state of conflict about the ultimate size of your goal, which is affecting your ability to create your mission statement, then why not make a calculated prediction and stick with it as a minimum, with serious intent. Then try to improve upon it as you come to a better understanding of your true capacity.

7. Are there some time partitions of crucial importance?

I have a very successful friend who celebrates major business events and milestones in his life by giving himself a special keepsake gift. The value of the gift often relates to the achievement quotient. Never over-look those important events in your life that signify the reaching of a place of importance. In times of discour-agement and disappointment, the quiet celebrations of personal victory can be used as an encouragement and a reminder of the struggles, victories and the milestones of the past. To assess the true partitions in respect to getting things done, or to reach a level of attainment of positioning that brings you closer towards your goals, will require planning your time.

Notes

Only adolescent dreamers believe that somehow everything falls into place effortlessly.

Why not divide your ultimate goal into several sections with time frames for specific attainment levels? What I am asking you to do is to treat the great gift called life seriously. If you ignore this great gift by your attitude towards time, then you will find to your embarrassment that no one else will treat your lifetime seriously either.

To help you to set some specific sections of your life into time and achievement partitions, consider the following exercise as a serious study. Conduct for your own benefit an in-depth geographical, political, demographical and world market needs analysis relative to your life goals, using some of the answers you have given to many of the questions already suggested in this book.

In conducting such a personal pursuit, bear in mind that those opportunities that are available today may fade and present an entirely different view of circumstances in just a few years. Laws that allow or prevent the merchandising of certain products because of national protection may also change in some countries, and changes in living standards with new perceived or real needs will open or close the opportunities that are currently available.

Many reports prepared for international organisations carry the responsibility of projecting possibilities fifty years into the future, which provokes some generalities together with some indisputable facts. If assessments with time partitions to allow for the future can and must be done by national and international organisations with all the variables and ramifications involved, then why shouldn't it be important for the individual? Your life and the journey you will take through life at different stages and ages, can impact the world if you are prepared to treat time partitions seriously!

8. **What specific payments are you prepared to make in time, talent and treasure?**

Knowing something of my schedule and world agenda, the most often asked question is, "What about your family?" The questioner anticipates that they have touched my Achilles heel and that the response will result in silence, excuses or double talk.

Earlier in my career I made some very simple, but lifelong commitments in respect to what price I would pay to reach what I believe to be my God-given life goals. One of those was not the loss or alienation of my family. Robina and I are still enjoying our marriage after over forty years together, and our children and grandchildren are all interactive and very close, which represents the nearest thing to heaven on earth for us. To raise and keep a family together in this modern, volatile world obviously does not necessarily mean staying at home 100% of the time, because simple statistics will soon show that being home every evening and weekend does not guarantee that your family relationships will always be right. Many broken

Notes

marriages and divided families will testify to that. I have found that what does work is an agreed agenda on the method and capacity of commitment to one another that never quits, with a deep abiding affection for each other. I would add another often ignored dynamic called faith.

There are of course other areas of my life that have caused some very heavy sacrifice, and I would counsel anyone who thinks that there are no sacrifices that have to be made to think again. To create talent requires time to study and the willingness to expose yourself to unpleasant experiences and the risk of financial loss, as you stretch towards the persistent, continued, relentless search for the key in your life that allows you to walk through that elusive door called success. I have never regretted the many sacrifices I have made, and continue to make, because what I receive in place of what I give up has eventually created a more meaningful place in the colourful parade of life.

If you accept the mantle of personal leadership you will be lonely, even in a crowd; you will be rejected even when you are right, and you will be plundered even when you have nothing left to give. Furthermore, you will feel the additional pain of comparing your own limited sacrifice with the anguish of others who are still in desperate need. The final payment is that you must give and keep on giving away all that you have earned, learned, aspired to and achieved to the next generation as a stepping stone for them.

Never discount the payment that you may have to make in your journey of life, and recognise its integral part in your "dynamic mission statement that works".

9. **Will it satisfy your inner yearnings?**

The idealism of youth expects much, wants much and has much to offer, but the object of the idealism changes as time and circumstances make their mark on the progress of young lives. Later on in life many things change, and in the ebb and flow of events, rarely does anything remain constant. One of the great mysteries of life is the continued quest, indecision and change that sets the human spirit towards something that today one would almost die for, yet it would receive nothing more than a cursory glance tomorrow.

From Homer to Chaucer through to contemporary authors, you can find in the literature of the ages that mankind has inner yearnings that are cherished and sought but rarely satisfied. What seems to be a desperate need for fulfilment, when acquired (and even before it is acquired) provokes yet another yearning that can be as all encompassing as the one before. Remember that you only have one life to give, and the allocation of talent and treasure are all limited by time, which beckons us forward towards our ultimate boundary. The messages the inner yearnings send to you always concern future possibilities; but they often presuppose, incorrectly, that the present circumstances will stay constant.

Try to keep a balance when seeking to satisfy your

Notes

inner yearnings, so that whatever the ultimate prize may be, it can in turn be used as a base or a launching pad toward something else. Your immediate inner yearnings, however grandiose, will always tend to reflect your present position.

I have found over a long life that the mind needs to be fed on a diet of information and inspiration to provoke it to perform well in the long term. But it will not continue to provide continued long term service without rewards. When that reward reflects itself in terms of rest, exhilaration, and humour it can restimulate the thoughts, energy and imagination just as a diet of good food stimulates the human frame. In contemplating your mission statement, bear in mind the style and the means in your journey through life towards ultimate goals. Your mission statement will need to reflect your deepest moral yearnings to ener-gise yourself towards the persistence necessary to get the job done. The unspoken yearnings relating to the way in which you want to be "well thought of" can only be satisfied by the actual strength of character you demonstrate throughout your mission, which will be assessed by those who observe your behaviour and attitude under all circumstances.

I have often been asked what the greatest stumbling block I have ever faced was. My response has always been the same.

My biggest problem is the person I see every morning when I look into the mirror and realise my own faults.

When writing your mission statement, use the moral base of your inner yearnings as a strong guide to be adhered to through the ups and downs of life. I am sure this will provide the stability needed to keep you on course during difficult and wonderful occasions.

Remember that each yearning usually provokes another, seeking to be quenched; but finding that illusive unquenchable quest and continuing towards its single theme is to touch, as it were, one of the wonderful secrets of life itself. To be swallowed up in its grasp will propel you towards achieving greatness.

10. At what time will it terminate without your continued input?

There are many examples of a quest continuing without the original instigator still being at the helm. Sometimes a younger or more adventurous person becomes involved and receives what in athletics is called "a second wind", and can continue something that was started by someone else, because the mission statement was so strong, directional and sure, and had the framework of clarity and inspiration. It is possible to continue a business or a personal goal over many generations. This can resemble a relay race with eager young runners ready to grasp the baton and swiftly continue to the next ambitious and capable person, who once again may set the pace.

Notes

Why discontinue the pursuit of your dreams when you retire, or because of dissatisfaction with your continued role? Why not programme your mission statement for permanence, which in the final analysis is the only real measure of sustaining value. If your ideas and goals are of value, then they may need to be pursued to their greatest permissible extent, even if you have become bored or are attracted to other opportunities.

Whilst many of us are sensitive to change (and most plans need to be adapted to the changes in opportunities), it requires a different and unselfish mind to think of a future not involving yourself, and so to extend your plans to include future generations.

It is a great pity to see major corporations and personal pursuits collapse because of the unlikely belief that there is no one else available to continue what is already up and running. My experience has shown me quite clearly that there are many eager younger men and women looking for a cause and an opportunity, or a vehicle they could develop into their life's work. They could well be blessed by tutoring from someone older who has the knowledge and the experience and is prepared to share it.

Why not plan your mission statement to be a living, continuing working document that can absorb the passages of time and encompass the changes of the market, as well as being an inspiration to the next generation to become involved, a statement which will provide ongoing sustenance to continue growth.

The tremendous waste in energy, ideas and time collectively over the last fifty years from projects started, stopped or faded through the lack of well-defined and continuing mission statements would be at least equal to that which could have created many gigantic sustaining global empires that could have made the world a better place to live. Take serious thought about using your life's brain power and energy towards a continuance, rather than a termination when your own energy fades; you will thereby put to extended use your original thrust.

As an additional thought, why not prepare your mission statement for longevity by considering the fact that change is inevitable and people, lifestyles, markets and laws are always in a continual process of change. Any mission statement that is to maintain its power during change must also take into account many of the unchanging principles that govern all human existence.

Beware of powerholders and manipulators, who always look for rules that they can apply to others, but avoid an agreed mission statement which has been designed for longevity and has, as its foundation, enduring principles that will help create a dynamic enterprise that will last long after the original initiator has gone. Do not commit energy towards something for which you have not created a mission statement which will continue, unless you deliberately want to waste your life.

Remember the only real measure of value is permanence.

Notes

CHAPTER FOUR

Creating a Mission Statement with Order

- *Describe yourself*
- *Describe your beliefs*
- *Describe your dreams*
- *Describe your pain transaction*
- *Describe your time frame*
- *Describe your specifics*

CHAPTER FOUR

Creating a Mission Statement With Order

Describe yourself

In a recent television interview some bystanders were asked to describe the person who had committed an offence that they had personally witnessed. It seemed that each person gave an entirely different description of the offender.

Wouldn't it be interesting if it were possible for twelve people who know you from different perspectives, such as someone you work with, another whom you have a competitive relationship with, and many others, to describe who you are as they see you. Better still, how would you objectively describe yourself so that others would nod in agreement and confirm your accurate assessment.

Most of us wear masks for different occasions and who we are can be determined very often by the circumstances we are in or the people we are out to impress. This may be very different from the person we really are to those whom we love and to those whom we don't feel so inclined to even like. The real assessment of who we really are needs to be measured in many ways and I would like to suggest just a few:

- the way we respond to a financial benefit or a loss

- our reaction to pressure

- meeting new people

- having to accept and respond to responsibility

- the attitude we have when we win

- the way we behave when we fail

- our feelings towards others worse off than us

- our subsequent actions towards them.

But I guess the most appropriate assessment of ourselves comes to us secretly as we lie awake at night and contemplate events that have recently occurred. We measure how we reacted or behaved against how we *should* have responded. The "could", "would" or "should have" responses unfortunately reflect the person that we are, and can also indicate, by contrast, a description of who we rather wistfully would like to be.

There are those rare times in our lives when reality supersedes pseudo-rationale, and we face ourselves as we really are. Seeing the fractures, we may well decide to programme some necessary reconstructive surgery on our personality.

If you want to get the most out of this book, then assess first the person that you really are against what you would actually like to be. Use the difference as a measurement for improvement. Any subterfuge in describing who you are will undoubtedly cause an incorrect target regarding who you want to be, and the outcome will be something less than what you really had in mind. The reality is that any misconception of who you are will translate itself into your mission statement and ma<e it almost impossible to fulfil and to achieve your ulximate goal, because the foundation is built on falsehood.

What I have just shared with you are practical and in-depth assessments to help you to discover who you are in respect to your behaviour and personality. This will provide the foundation not only for a mission statement but for your relationships and successes throughout your entire life.

Describing yourself also means a description of that other entity, which is your business or organisation, and the truth and clarity with which it is done will also provide a sound basis for your mission statement and

---

Notes

growth. Why not try some further assessments and add some of your own thoughts to help you evaluate yourself or your organisation, and so provide a basis for a dynamic mission statement that works.

Describe your beliefs

Deep seated beliefs always work their way to the surface and penetrate and direct our action at all levels and in all circumstances. Beliefs can at times be suppressed, changed, even exaggerated, or minimised during conversation or under stress. But that which we inwardly hold as our personal beliefs will ultimately surface and direct our thoughts, and ultimately our actions throughout our life. It is sad, but true, that very few people have seriously examined the basis for their beliefs because they obtain them from others as they develop. They have therefore accepted peer influence or what others believed, and unfortunately adopt it as part of their own personality and expression instead of as a basis for assessment to build their own life upon.

Consider seriously your beliefs in respect to the inevitability of events. Do you believe that *life is really choices or chances?*

A simple understanding of personal accountability for one's own actions in regard to choices puts you at the helm of responsibilities, whereas the belief in the inevitability of events can leave you open to the continued acceptance of that which you are presented with in life, against what you can *choose* to do. Obviously there are things in life that are inevitable and there are those that are matters of choice. But the questions need to be answered in respect to the predominant belief factor in each case.

- Do you believe that opportunities come to you?

- Or do you have to seek them out?

- Or do you believe in both of those statements, and if so, how do you clearly identify the balance between them?

- What is your belief about the future of your country and, in fact, the future of the world in the areas of economics, safety and human standards which will have an effect upon your future and that of your family?

- Have you ever considered the basic belief that you have in your own abilities to cope with the future world? Are you basing that belief on past performance and predicated personal changes you will make to your life, or is it just a hope?

- Do your political beliefs follow a particular party or do you have your own personal criteria for economic, legal and human standards of government behaviour and intervention?

Notes

- Have you considered the question of God and if so can you describe the God you believe in?

- Can you give authoritative evidence to support such a belief which will provide a living philosophy to sustain you in the ups and downs of life?

Commitment to a value system of beliefs will assist you in every area of your life towards a more peaceful, directional and confident future.

Describe your dreams

Most dreams are fuzzy or general, and even when specific they often lack the descriptive means of assessment. In many cases a dream is verbalised but not documented, which allows the possessor of the dream to vary its objectives at every description and thereby lose the power of specifics. In doing so, the dream is assigned to the byway of fantasy. The evidence seems to be that if you have problems in describing your dream in attainable and measurable form, then you will have multiple problems in realising your dream. When you dream, you are on the threshold of creation because a dream expresses more than just a thought; it encompasses the activity of the imagination, the hopes and desires of the ego, the capacity of the mind and the thrust and stimulation of the spirit. A dream transforms something that was not conscious to something which is now conscious and has the possibility of reality.

What is often overlooked when declaring and assessing your dream is the cost or value of exchange.

Let me explain. If you have a serious life dream or even a long term dream, then you are prepared in effect to trade your life for it. The rate of exchange for your life in the realisation of a dream must reflect the value you place on your life span, because that is practically what you exchange for the fulfilment of your dream. The cost of a big dream, a small dream, or even no dream, is the same. It is the right to exchange your mortal life for something, and you can give no more and eventually no less than life itself before you depart from this planet.

Consider of course the expandability of your dream because a dream can be expanded as it grows with you, and can even stimulate mental and spiritual growth beyond what you originally had in mind. Always be conscious of the fact that when you dream, you are on the periphery of God-likeness. In a sense you become a mini-creator when you in a very real way create something out of nothing.

Describe your pain transaction

One of the greatest thinkers of all time was so engrossed in the process of learning that in the middle of the icy winters in Europe, with only a little heating available, he would have a dish of ice water under the

---

Notes

table at night to place his bare feet in if he started to doze off to sleep during his study period.

A great pianist was once approached by an admirer who said, "I would do anything to be able to play the piano like you . . ." In response the pianist said, "No, you wouldn't".

At 26 years of age and almost illiterate, I spent night after night, year in and year out, practising articulation, and learning and absorbing helpful material. During a 15 year period I met regularly with a small group of men for two hours each week for prayer and Bible study which today provides a foundation for all I am and all that I hope to be. I still get approached by people throughout the world seeking the secrets of success. In a nutshell I would like to share one of those secrets with you and it is this: "Success is the willingness to bear pain".

Not as a masochist or just to prove you can endure, but rather, if necessary, in the process of becoming what you would like to be.

Pain comes from failure, disappointment, embarrassment and the continuing thrust to achieve your goals, often facing setbacks and major changes in events, which can put you further behind from even where you really started. The pain of success can continue day after day, month after month, and year after year from trying to uncover, through the camouflage of information, that which conceals your key to success. Pain is not being able to get out of yourself that which you know you can produce.

Generally mankind is seduced to the comfort zone — but victories are rarely found in the comfort zone. As a matter of fact, it appears that most achievers in any field have been in the pain arena.

Beware of the camouflage of mediocrity, which knows the edge of success, but never ventures past the still waters of safety and comfort.

Do you buckle under during stress? Is confrontation avoided? Do you avoid discomfort to the detriment of your performance?

Seeking to avoid confrontation or discomfort is natural, and will provide protection from harm — but the possibility of success in any field presupposes that conflict, opposition, competition and difficulties will always arise. If you find that is not for you, it may indicate that "followership" rather than leadership is the best course for you to take.

For those of you who have aspirations towards leadership in any field, I would suggest that you be mindful of the fact that leadership presupposes that there will be "followership", and often we need to understand the ethos of "followership" before we can become a good leader.

Describe your time frame

How would you feel if a surgeon or the pilot of a jumbo jet guesstimated about time frames regarding the possibility of a major mistake? What would you say if your business colleagues refused to accept the restraints of a simple wrist watch? In what circum-

---

Notes

stances do you think we would find ourselves if nature abandoned its orchestration of time relating to the seasons?

Our whole existence is based on time and timing. Yet we often tend to overlook this universal law when considering our achievement quotient because we believe we can somehow override its predictable boundaries.

To create a mission statement that works predicates a time frame to reach our destinations, and any attempt to ignore the fundamentals of these laws is folly. There are, of course, many instances in life where the time frames to achieve certain tasks have been beaten, just as there are those times when the time frames have been inadequate for any number of reasons. The essence of our time frame in *how to create a dynamic mission statement that works* is to plan the journey so that we can predict with reasonable surety our performance.

Each part of the journey is a unit in the whole and provides building blocks towards the completed construction, which has as its ultimate end reaching your desired goal. Sometimes (particularly when we are young) in the haste to reach a specific goal, the mission statement is cut to such bare essentials that the final destination, when achieved, is so poorly supported it can be in danger of collapse.

The other dangerous alternative is that, in haste to reach the final goal, many important signals and obstacles are ignored or overlooked. The critical path to a successful conclusion is missed and inevitable failure may result.

Describe your specifics

In creating your *dynamic mission statement that works*, clear targets need to be assessed which are regarded as being of paramount importance for the journey. They need to be put into written form, ready for action.

So far many of the areas we have been describing require some attention. Now some very serious questions in respect to our target must be asked.

For instance, think about the goal that you want. Is it fixed or can it be moved geographically due to economic, political, and even seasonal factors? What is the numerical measurement that makes the goal complete? Let us look just for a moment at the goal that creates the mission statement.

Limits:

The ultimate goal must have some limits even if they have to be created, because without limits any final destination is obscure. With no specific limits you have no specific target.

A no-limit entity may be alright for a rare, unusual abundant opportunity where at every turn fresh gains can be made, but it becomes more a reaction rather

Notes

than a prepared action and is very difficult to sustain because of its capacity to create boredom and sloppiness. This type of unusual opportunity generally has a limited time frame so the ultimate destination finally has to be reckoned with.

Another very interesting question to consider is, "How are the limits set?" Are they based on supposition? Or are they based on provable calculations?

Liabilities:

There is an old but very sound dictum that says, "Look before you leap". It is good personal and business advice. Consider with all seriousness the liabilities, corporate and personal, that could impede the progress of your journey. On a personal basis, it does not take much brilliance to suggest that if you are only five feet tall you are going to find it difficult to become a world-class basketball player.

In any journey there are many seen and unseen obstacles that need to be overcome and minimising their presence is not going to be helpful. Assess the reality of what you are up against, and create a sure fire plan for overcoming every known obstacle and you will make the possibilities of success more sure.

Obstacles can be overcome. One that I have had to deal with many times is my complete colour blindness; but it did not prevent me from selling paint or ladies' fashion in my early years, because I could remember the numbers on the colour tags and thereby trade with complete confidence.

Carefully lay out all the obstacles and create a plan to overcome all difficulties. In the long run you will find that the hours of deep, concentrated, investigative thought will save you light years of time on the job. Consider also an emergency plan for when unforeseen obstacles appear — it could take the form of a reality countdown with logical problem solving steps that will fall into place automatically.

Longevity:

Creating a goal for longevity means creating a mission statement for longevity, because any journey will include maintenance and management to keep the goal from collapsing from lack of attention. A laissez-faire attitude towards long-term planning in business and personal life goes against the blatant evidence of longevity which declares its prominence in every modern city throughout the entire world, that is, the proliferation of insurance buildings and the size of their investment portfolio. Let me explain. Insurance companies are prepared to gamble on the length of your life and they calculatingly bet against your worst fears by providing security for your most precious possession — your life. The evidence is clear that the insurance companies believe that you will have longevity and they usually win. So why not at least agree with a proven rule and accept that the possibility of long life is a reality. Organisations are commenced

---

Notes

and maintained by people, and therefore they can also have the benefits of longevity.

So why not think, plan, buy, build, save and create your own dynamic mission statement that works for longevity with all of the philosophy, culture and principles that have been shared in this book?

CHAPTER FIVE

Putting Your Personal Mission Statement Together

Now we come to the finale of creating your own "dynamic mission statement that works". We will put into mechanical form all the facets of the mission statement so that it becomes a specific, practical and durable document.

CHAPTER FIVE

Putting Your Personal Mission Statement Together

Now we come to the finale of creating your own *dynamic mission statement that works*. We will put into mechanical form all the facets of the mission statement so that it becomes a *specific, practical and durable document*.

Getting the pieces together:

Why not put a price on your life?:

During the early days of Australia and the wild west of America, there were outlaws who literally had a price on their head, and their posters usually carried the additional slogan: "Dead or Alive". It appeared to the lawmakers and the government of the day that it was not only possible but very practical to assess in dollar terms the value of a person who caused trouble of a certain magnitude. The price put on their lives would be based on the value of not having that person around any more. In simple terms, it could be said that these people had a removal value that was related to a monetary amount.

Some time ago at a seminar in a very poor area in the United States, I decided to conduct an assessment of a very different kind with an unusual experiment. I sought out the poorest and most discouraged person in attendance. This person's situation was appalling. She was impoverished, abused, abandoned and the object of many misfortunes; but she readily agreed to step into the starring role in this seminar experiment in an effort to improve her lot. In the large hall you could have heard a pin drop as she responded to my questions about her life and experiences, and her foreboding for the future. As she and many others wept, it became difficult for me to focus on the task as I saw it before me. But knowing full well that I had a job to do, I pressed on. After a considerable time of attending to her regrets, remorse and self-flagellation, I decided to make my move. I wrote on a huge whiteboard the word "physical", and then asked Emily this simple question: "If you had to sell your physical strength for manual labour for a lifetime, what price would you put upon it?" The crowd waited in anticipation as Emily wrestled with the question, and then she responded with a large monetary amount and quickly added, "It would be worth at least that figure". I entered the amount alongside the word "physical". I then wrote the word "mental" on the whiteboard and asked what she would sell her mental capacity for. Then I followed in the same manner with the words "heritage", "family", "dreams", finally closing with the price of her soul, which to her meant an abandonment towards her creator — only to be firmly told: "That is priceless and not negotiable". As we quickly added up all the amounts Emily had put down in dollar terms, not including her soul, it was indeed an impressive fortune. The most noticeable surprise came not from the large financial assessment of Emily's personal asset reserve but the incredible change in her attitude, deportment and countenance. Emily had changed, and I believe it will be permanent because she now knows something of her own true value.

Why don't *you* estimate your own value in dollar terms to give you a better perspective before you create your own dynamic mission statement that works.

Check Your Immediate Assets:

After having dealt with your personal value, it is now time to evaluate other assets you have, but may not be fully aware of. The most obvious place to start is the country or location that you live in and its acceptance and accessibility and importance to the logistical requirements for your mission. Another item of paramount importance is your time in the history of the world, with its fast communications and technology, which was not available at a previous time in history. Your age must be evaluated in relationship to the

---

Notes

length of the journey and the stamina required, together with your present abilities and mobility, which may assist you in your quest.

Clarify Your Goals:

The important requirement here is to know what your ultimate goal is, because without a goal your target is vague. Knowing your goal provokes a need for a journey to possess it. Hence, your dynamic mission statement that works.

The elements of goal setting can be simple in expression, but like a mission statement, they become more involved when it comes to actually qualifying them and writing them down.

THE GOALS FORMULA:
(As described in my book *How to Reach Your Life Goals*).

1. Define your goal
It must be measurable, and specific, and if you do not already have a goal, then make finding a goal your goal.

2. Set out your strategy
If you can't measure it then of course you can't manage it. Here we really are talking about your mission statement.

3. **Plan out your problems**

This covers all problems, and dealing with them must be a part of your mission statement. Problems include personal and mechanical ones. Problems always beg solutions and solutions always create growth.

4. **Build in reserves**

Reserves must be built in to the ultimate goal to prevent collapse. But they also must be built into the mission as a protection against losing any ground that has already been gained.

5. **Relate to time frames**

Just as a time frame needs to be assessed against the ultimate goal, so must time frames be locked in for crucial staging points of the mission journey.

6. **Create a master plan**

In creating a master plan for goal setting, which includes the ultimate goal and all its ramifications, the linchpin must be the mission statement, because a mission statement provides the sustaining thrust to get the job done.

Notes

7. **Start today**

Just as it takes a large amount of fuel to launch a rocket, so it takes more energy and resolve to get started on your goal and your mission statement. But a different quality and quantity is required once it is off the ground.

Why not stop for a moment and think of all the things you were going to start many years ago but never seemed to get around to. Measure that against what you actually did commence and then against what you continued to complete. Without a doubt it will show you that those that weren't started with good planning and gusto, usually didn't end up getting finished.

The other areas to reconsider are intangibles such as the kind of lifestyle you want to develop (do not disregard this very important area of consideration because it will or will not place you within a sphere of influence that could affect your whole future) within the boundaries of your mission statement. Also choose areas of your personality that you want to enhance or subdue to make your journey smoother and more enjoyable. Remember continually that a mission is a journey and usually long-term. So the more clearly you plan it, the less obstacles you will encounter.

Priority Requirements:

Whatever the final goal is to be and whatever quantity or quality the mission is to become, the most obvious and yet the most overlooked requirement is a permanent cash flow vehicle. Once a permanent cash flow vehicle is created, it can be expanded with the mission. This gives the goal a secure basis.

This permanent cash flow is often overlooked when academic, charitable or sporting goals are involved, which places the initiator into the uncertainty of seeking outside support or begging others for funds, which in the final analysis can be just as time consuming and certainly more precarious than creating your own permanent cash flow, because when you create your own cash flow you are in complete control.

A cash flow can be quickly created by selling on a commission basis, or becoming a principal agent for a product or selling some kind of service that fits in with the style and direction you are going, or simply by working for someone else.

(Remember, that commission is always created for mediocrity, so that the average person can make a living — and any one who thinks and perseveres can easily beat that and make a small fortune.)

The ultimate way to create a cash flow is to save some income continually and finally have enough funds invested to be able to live comfortably from the interest, leaving more time to clarify your future with the finances on auto-pilot. The other more practical alternative is to make the mission economically productive within itself, thus gaining the increase in funds, as it becomes successful, to meet all growth needs.

Notes

Eight Steps to Personal Achievement:

As in any successful achievement there are some rules that need to be applied to obtain predictable results.

The following eight steps to personal achievement are a well tried and proven method that has been tested over many years. The creating of your *dynamic mission statement that works* is but a part of the overall formula and I will show you here how it fits into a dynamic plan.

To obtain the full benefit of these eight steps, each part of the formula must be dealt with thoroughly. Each step will be explained with particular emphasis on the mission statement, which is the theme and purpose of this book and a major cause for misunderstanding in the success process. You must focus clearly on the *process* and accept that the project can be altered to suit individual requirements. Any inadequacies in the progress of your achievements will quickly show up in the four following areas.

- Your goal was not fully, specifically, and measurably defined.

- Your mission statement lacked investigative research and documentation.

- Your commitment level was lacking in deep thought and sustained directive action.

- Your relationship between your mission statement and your goal was vague.

Now we will list, very simply, the eight steps to personal achievement in preparation for your personal mission statement.

1. The goal

2. The vehicle

3. The creed

4. The commitment

5. The qualification

6. The positioning

7. The assessment

8. The destination

We will deal with each one of these separately.

Notes

1. The Goal

The setting of a goal is only the first process toward any predictable achievement. The illustrative goal that I am going to present to you here may be far from what you have in mind, but the steps to any significant personal quest must first of all have a destination (the goal) and the transportation (the mission) to ensure that the destination will indeed be arrived at. The key to this illustration is to follow the process and not the project, and so the process of creating *a dynamic mission statement that works* will develop into a simple management formula which aims with some certainty at the ultimate success of your goal. The suggested goal is as follows.

The Goal — Suggested Mission Statement

To build within the next twenty years an international business empire which will provide $100 million in surplus funds for my benevolent pursuits.

Date: Signed:

2. Discovering Your Vehicle

To make any journey possible, there must be a vehicle that can carry the load relative to the goal. The mission's role, of course, is to mobilise the vehicle towards the goal — hence the choice of a vehicle must be adaptable to the goal. For instance, it would not be compatible to have a vehicle that restricted travel if your goal demanded international markets, or conversely, to have a vehicle demanding international travel when your goal is primarily local. So, in short, the vehicle must be subject to the goal, and the mission has the task of energising the vehicle to the goal. It must be obvious by now that the vehicle is another part of the structure that requires careful selection, because it will directly influence both the speed and the style of the mission. A simple question should be asked when considering your vehicle. For instance, if the vehicle that you are using as your business has to do with oil then you need to make the long term decision as to whether or not you are in the oil business or the energy business, because eventually electricity and some hitherto unknown energy units will be discovered and a decision you initially make could lead to the obsolescence of future opportunities. A suggested mission statement entry for your vehicle could be:

The Vehicle — Suggested Mission Statement

The vehicle by which I reach my goal will always be the focus of my financial multiplication and the protection by which all decisions must be tempered.

Notes

3. The Creed

Here you will need to use all the information that you have gathered about yourself during the study of this book. You will notice that each area is sectionalised to give you a clearer formula covering all the aspects necessary to equip yourself to form and write a plan for this journey. It will require that "The Creed" expresses some personal desires that hopefully will remain constant throughout your life. The character beliefs and intangibles will provide for you at all times throughout your mission the sustaining thrust to continue against what would seem insurmountable odds whilst still retaining those attributes of morality which will promote and provide an anchor in the stormy seas of life.

The Creed — Suggested Mission Statement

I am a person of "destiny" and I know what I am prepared to exchange my life for, and I herein declare my mission to reach my ultimate goal. I will always maintain a positive temperament and present myself in speech, dress, behaviour and lifestyle as a distinctive major player in the arena of life. Loyalty and commitment to my family and friends will be my continuing asset, and my quest for knowledge and information to meet my needs and weaknesses will be met by a discipline of an equal measure.

4. The Commitment

This is in the area of discipline and growth and is usually the area of break-down. To sum it up quite simply, it is a matter of integrity. There is no honour in making commitments and later breaking them. This part of your mission statement is the essence of what really happens, and without the desperation to fulfil this part of your mission statement, all else is futile. In very clear terms it simply means fulfilling the substance of every part of your mission statement, and turning good thoughts and emotion into power. (As an interesting side issue here, the biblical word for God's love to man is "agape", which is a discipline not dependent on emotion.)

I could name scores of friends and acquaintances who started on the road to success bright-eyed and full of great dreams, enthusiasm and optimism, only to fall by the way side because they did not commit themselves to the price that needed to be paid to finish the course. The pain you will endure in your commitment is unavoidable. Bear it and weakness will exit from your character and mission.

Notes

The Commitment — Suggested Mission Statement

My commitment to complete my mission is as sacred to me as life itself, and is accepted as a great gift of power. So I will make commitments carefully with the understanding that all that I am and hope to be will be embodied in this great treasure.

5. The Qualifications

The qualifications that would be necessary to reach the suggested goal would be many, but could loosely be described in the following way. To build a *large* business enterprise starts with learning to build a successful business on a *small* scale. This would provide the nett profits to do in a small way what you ultimately want to do on a larger scale at a later date. A working knowledge of economics and accountancy will give the theory, but the successful working out of the theory in practical terms will provide the inescapable proof that you are in fact ready to go on to a higher grade.

Assess the qualifications you need relative to your goal to enable you to create the mission to reach it, always acknowledging that there will be unknowns and new developments. At all costs, avoid jumping into areas that you have not proven by experience. Carefully study each step to ensure that no ground will be lost by moving out into the unknown without reserves.

The Qualifications — Suggested Mission Statement

I will enrich my life by learning the lessons of economics, management and entrepreneurship by exposing myself to continuing higher levels of practical and theoretical understanding. When I cannot prove by substance my lessons, I will repeat them until I can, until by automatic response I will use the principles that I have found that work. My financial reserves will prevent me from losing too much ground should I make a mistake or should misfortune come upon me. The eight points of my dynamic mission statement that works will always be subject to qualification and understanding and any fracture or infringement will be promptly corrected. All my qualifications will be assessed and scrutinised under the clear light of two inseparable qualities, truth and proof, seeking always to minimise my mistakes by maximising my clarity.

6. The Positioning

This part of your dynamic mission statement that works deals with positioning yourself in the parade of life to assist you to play a major role in the acquisition

Notes

of your goal. It must be obvious that if you remove yourself from where the action is, then you are going to find it difficult to be successful. Do not overlook creating friendships and allies that you may find useful and interesting as you grow, and try to deal with people you respect or even like, which makes the length of the journey more pleasant. Seek to place yourself in a crucial role wherever information relative to your challenge becomes easier to obtain. As an information receiver, you automatically become an informed centre of influence. As part of your environment structure, pay attention to your permanent location and travel schedule, seeking to develop second and third person influence which will enhance your real and perceived interests. Be just as careful in avoiding involvement that would conflict with your Creed. By doing so, you will send a clear picture of who you are, what you stand for and where you intend to go.

The Positioning — Suggested Mission Statement

I will seek to position myself at the pivotal point of progress and change, always maintaining the strength stability gives and sensitive to how it can be of benefit towards the achievement of my mission. My friendships and liaisons will reflect and enhance my direction, location and mobility, always seeking to place me in timing and opportunity in the most crucial position. A careful selection of people, places and events will represent at all times my desire to influence and to be influenced towards my objectives.

7. The Assessment

Real measurements will need to be undertaken to assess the progress of your mission at regular intervals. The agreed goal has within itself specifics and measurements which must be broken down into quantitative time frames to evaluate progress. Sometimes the assessment may be more tangible, such as positions; at other times the progress may be more a matter of influence or positioning, ready to produce more tangible assets later. Each of your mission moves must reflect progress towards your destination, otherwise the estimated time of arrival may never come. To suggest a dynamic mission statement that works without any form of regular assessment is to invite failure and may give the impression of activity without objectivity.

The Assessment — Suggested Mission Statement

My mission has monthly time, substance and information checks in direct relationship to progress, all calculated in numerical terms to avoid inaccuracies. I will always pay particular attention to personal growth assessments and spheres of influence

Notes

that are needed to reach each point of my assessment. Major checks in all areas will be conducted on an annual basis, and five year objectives will be carefully created so that they are reflected in quarterly segments in the overall mission.

8. The Destination

No journey can be completed without knowing and focusing on the destination. The whole purpose of creating your dynamic mission statement that works is to arrive at a predetermined destination (called a goal) in a measurable and specific way, within a timetable that was predetermined. A clear look at the destination and its exact time, shape and form needs to be clearly visible in the mind of the missioner to keep you on course and to prevent points of deviation. One of the unusual aspects of life is that we sometimes get more than we aim for because the person that commences the mission is unaware of the personal changes that will take place in their capabilities and capacities, hence, sometimes the destination (the goal) can finish up being much larger than that which was predetermined.

The Destination — Suggested Mission Statement

Realising that my focus must be twofold, that is, on the clarity of the final goal and the mission to achieve it, I must also sense and enhance the growth in the personal qualities that will assist both the mission and the goal.

Always bear in mind that this is *your* mission. It depends totally upon your dedication and should not be subject to events or the expectation of other people. The "take charge" lifestyle commenced at the beginning of this book must be constant. If you have any doubts or uncertainties at this point, then you should go back to the beginning of this book and with a marker, go through each chapter as a renewed lesson about your journey in life.

THE SUGGESTED PERSONAL GOAL

To build within the next twenty years an international business empire to provide $100 million in surplus funds for my benevolent pursuits.

Date: Signed:

Notes

COMPLETED PERSONAL
MISSION STATEMENT

The vehicle by which I reach my goal will always be the focus of my financial multiplication and the protection by which all decisions must be tempered.

I am a person of "destiny" and I know what I am prepared to exchange my life for, and I herein declare my mission to reach my ultimate goal. I will always maintain a positive temperament and present myself in speech, dress, behaviour and lifestyle as a distinctive major player in the arena of life. Loyalty and commitment to my family and friends will be my continuing asset, and my quest for knowledge and information to meet my needs and weaknesses will be met by a discipline of an equal measure.

My commitment to complete my mission is as sacred to me as life itself, and is accepted as a great gift of power. So I will make commitments carefully with the understanding that all that I am and hope to be will be embodied in this great treasure.

I will enrich my life by learning the lessons of economics, management and entrepreneurship by exposing myself to continuing higher levels of practical and theoretical understanding. When I cannot prove by substance my lessons, I will repeat them until I can, until by automatic response I will use the principles that I have found that work. My financial reserves will prevent me from losing too much ground should I make a mistake or should misfortune come upon me.

The eight points of my dynamic mission statement that works will always be subject to qualification and understanding and any fracture or infringement will be promptly corrected. All my qualifications will be assessed and scrutinised under the clear light of two inseparable qualities, truth and proof, seeking always to minimise my mistakes by maximising my clarity.

I will seek to position myself at the pivotal point of progress and change, always maintaining the strength stability gives and sensitive to how it can be of benefit towards the achievement of my mission. My friendships and liaisons will reflect and enhance my direction, location and mobility, always seeking to place me in timing and opportunity in the most crucial position. A careful selection of people, places and events will represent at all times my desire to influence and to be influenced towards my objectives.

My mission has monthly time, substance and information checks in direct relationship to progress, all calculated in numerical terms to avoid inaccuracies. I will always pay particular attention to personal growth assessments and spheres of influence that are needed to reach each point of my assessment.

Notes

Major checks in all areas will be conducted on an annual basis and five-year objectives will be carefully created so that they are reflected in quarterly segments in the overall mission.

Realising that my focus must be twofold, that is, on the clarity of the final goal and the mission to achieve it I must also sense and enhance the growth in the personal qualities that will assist in both the mission and the goal.

Date: Signed:

Putting Your Corporate Mission Statement Together

A corporation faces a different kind of scrutiny, with dependence placed more on the team than the individual.

CHAPTER SIX

Putting Your Corporate Mission Statement Together

In this part of our study together we will move from the singular into the multiple regarding people, opportunities, complications and variables.

What we as individuals may wish to do must now be tempered by what we can accomplish through others, including bureaucracy and the barriers it builds, as well as the force it can be for progress if at the commencement the plans for stimulation and growth are built in.

Whilst many of the steps towards a personal and corporate mission statement are similar, they will differ in content because one deals primarily with an individual while the other is a separate and distinctive entity, known as a corporation or organisation. A corporation faces a different kind of scrutiny, with dependence placed more on the team than the individual. In placing the emphasis on the team, I am not suggesting that all are equally responsible, but rather that the leader of that team must provide a climate in which all participants can become part of the whole. When talent and desire coincide in an individual, then that person can be fulfilled by being fully stretched.

Getting the pieces together

The following ten points will provide a simple benchmark that will allow you in an organised way to pull the elementary threads together in preparation for creating your corporate mission statement that works.

1. Clarity of direction

2. Care and understanding of human nature

3. Comprehensive study of markets and trends

4. Tenacity for both quality and growth

5. Knowledge of short and long term economics

6. Vision for new concepts and developments

7. Commitment to the long term challenge

8. Ability to cope with continued criticism and loneliness

9. Preparedness to give others the credit

10. Selection of directors

1. **Clarity of Direction**

The mission you are about to commence is like any journey and it must have absolute clarity of direction. As you prepare to write out a corporate mission statement, the objective is that *the people at the lowest level of involvement must understand in unmistakable terms what is meant and how they personally fit in to the overall plan.* Any ambiguity of any kind will provide a toe-hold for misunderstanding and mistakes which can burn up time, money and trust that will inevitably sabotage progress.

Clarity of direction provides a security blanket for those who do not have the positioning or the privilege to be involved in the major decision making that controls their very livelihoods. For a medium or large organisation the assurance of clarity will pay large economic dividends because the work force knows the road ahead. Without mixed signals, there is very little wastage of energy.

2. **Care and understanding of human nature**

All of us have heard the stories of people who have worked tirelessly for a long time with a company and were convinced that they were the linchpins holding the whole place together, only to receive little or no

---

Notes

appreciation for their loyalty, talent and effort. Some leave, only to find that the gap was quickly filled, while others seek and find a bigger and better opportunity, leaving the previous employer floundering.

In general terms, people can be divided into four distinct groups:

(a) *Maintenance*
Those who want a secure job without responsibility.

(b) *Stabilisers*
Those who desire some form of medium level of responsibility and are prepared to work for it.

(c) *Destabilisers*
These can be found at every level. They move from job to job seeking to enhance their talents and provide them to the highest bidder. They can be very helpful for a short time, but become restless and must move on.

(d) *Growth*
These people distinguish themselves by their commitment, intelligence, and their hunger to accept responsibility and new challenges.

Careful understanding and appreciation for the special needs of each of these groups will unify them towards the mission, and, in doing so, provide a power force of awesome dimensions.

3. Comprehensive study of markets and trends

In the creating of your corporate or organisation mission statement, you will require at least a working knowledge of markets and trends. I would like to add another two important elements, particularly if you are going to market internationally, and that is culture and law.

To know your market and how you can possess it proves the often quoted, and I believe true, statement that "nothing continually happens in business until something is sold". Whatever your goal is to be, its final success will be to a large degree dependent on a comprehensive understanding of markets and trends. So often a market that appears to be strong and in full flight can collapse because insufficient attention was paid to the trend in respect to styles, obsolescence or marketing strategies. Attention must also be paid to immediate start-up markets and trends, with a further serious focus on future innovative trends.

When moving into fresh markets, even in your own country, beware of possible cultural and legal differences that may impede or even prevent market share. This information can easily be obtained from the appropriate Government Departments of the country where your interests are, or from tourist, migration, Government investment or political literature.

Notes

4. Tenacity for both quality and growth

One would expect the simple desire for quality would naturally guarantee growth. But economic history has shown quite clearly that business has very few guarantees, and the best product may have other short-comings. For instance, if the quality of your product causes it to be too expensive, or the delivery is not consistent, or the advertising and the outlets are inadequate, or it is too far ahead of its time, then the capacity for growth is very much diminished. There has to be a balanced pattern of price, quality, availability and awareness to ensure that quality and quantity are best exploited. To start and stop a market mid-stream because attention has not been paid to all of these elements will cause considerable expense and difficulties. It will also have a negative effect on those in your organisation; interruptions signal insecurity and uncertain, temporary progress to them.

The aggressiveness of the corporation will keep it on the cutting edge of growth, and the added ingredient of quality will ensure it remains there. It comes from the top down, not from the bottom up. The mission statement and the provocateur (which is the missioner) must possess in reliable and demonstrative terms the permanent appetite for quality and growth to achieve success.

5. Knowledge of short and long term economics

It has often been said that "if you put a salesman in the same room as an accountant, you can be assured of conflict". The other cliché about those who handle the business accounts is that "they do not kick the goals, they only keep the score". In spite of what is said, I believe we need to be reminded in business that a good accountant with a short and long term in-depth knowledge of economics can often clear the fiscal pathway ahead, alerting you to danger signals and preventing ground already claimed from being lost.

The best kind of economic advice for you to obtain is from those who are already demonstratively rich and have maintained that position over a long term.

What often seems to be a good economic strategy today can turn into an economic nightmare tomorrow. So here are some simple but effective economic principles that I have found both protective and expansive for any business.

(1) Maintain control and do not relinquish it at any price.

(2) Beware of economic involvement where debt can expand through fluctuating currencies, interest rates or penalties.

(3) Always protect the gains that you have made.

(4) Never risk your future on the prospects of a loan.

Notes

(5) Always have protective capital reserves.

6. Vision for new concepts and development

There are some rare businesses that have survived by doing the same thing, the same way over several generations. But during the passage of time their market diminishes, and their products or services are no longer required. You will find that changes in lifestyles, materials and new products finally make them obsolete. Any mission that does not seek out by investigative development, new ways, new uses and/or alternative products is doomed to failure and cannot stand the test of time.

Create an atmosphere of innovation by encouraging adventure within the organisation, even to the point of holding special meetings at every level of employment for that purpose.

Many times I have seen management wrestle with problems that they are too close to, only to find that someone in the lower echelons of the corporation easily provides the answer.

Develop an attitude of openness to ideas and a reward system for those that are useful. Bear in mind that the methods of today are not necessarily the methods of tomorrow, although there are those rare occasions when you can even go back to the past and resurrect an old method and by adaptation and innovation make it useful again. The key here is to look into the future and try to visualise what will be needed and how that need can be met.

7. Commitment to the long term challenge

A personal mission statement allows you time to relax and even drift for a while; but the corporate mission does not possess that luxury. A corporate mission statement automatically has within its tightly held boundaries certain restrictions that need to be assessed against a long term commitment that will affect the life of the leader in particular, and in a slightly lesser way those in the upper echelons of management.

Because of the responsibility to creditors and to the market place, large businesses cannot go into neutral for a respite as an individual can. The commitment that the corporation has to those they employ, which, I believe, is a sacred trust, means that vigilance must be the watch word at all times. Just as some new employees commence their work today, so retirees are relinquishing their work at the same time, and so the process continues, with each trusting the company's mission as expressed in the mission statement for them to keep their commitment to their own families and their mortgages. What a committed mission can do is to put a kinder face on capitalism, and in the process everyone benefits.

Notes

8. **Ability to cope with continued criticism and loneliness**

The leader (the missioner) as an individual will always be the object of criticism and may often feel somewhat lonely because of the authoritative position he/she holds, which automatically creates isolation. A corporate mission statement comes into its own in these two areas. It provides a known direction which minimises criticism, and has the allegiance of an agreed group of people, which provides something of the comfort of a crowd all aiming at the same target. Often the management and the whole group will close ranks to protect others from criticism because they see not only the person involved inflicted but the reflection it has on the total corporation.

A leader who sticks to the principles of the corporate mission statement, in the face of outside opposition, may even find him/or herself suddenly given hero status because the group feels that, in standing up for the mission, they themselves have been protected. Never underestimate group power and support when a mission statement is adhered to, even if it has by its implications created some negative results. The fact is that if it is maintained it will produce security and confidence.

9. **Preparedness to give others the credit**

A mission statement that does not recognise the efforts of all will not get all the effort. The operation of a corporation must always be recognised as a team effort, while not minimising in any way the role of the leader or leaders. The essence of good leadership is to accurately give direction, continued motivation, long term planning; and then become the hero by giving away a great deal of the credit to others on the team. In no way does this diminish the public stature of the leader or leaders but it can enhance it, and if they have a limited public personality, it provides the mystique that ultimately sets them apart. The best response to any successful corporate campaign by the leader is, without exception, to point to all the team players, even naming individuals if special distinctions need to be made. Loyalty always follows genuine appreciation.

10. Selection of directors

I am of the belief that there should be two board levels to address the stability, policy making, fiscal responsibility and planning of every corporation. The first group should have the legal power and the responsibility for the total operation. In my opinion, these should be people with a diversity of interests and professions that are already in possession of their own successful corporations with a long term track record. Rarely do I consider business people who have retired because they have a dinosaur's reaction to time, and their decisions usually reflect that. I almost never have

---

Notes

on the legal board of directors those who are employed by others, irrespective of how high up a ladder they are, because (a) their time is not their own and (b) they are not used to making plans and decisions with their own money.

The second group of directors should be an advisory board with no legal or company responsibilities. This may include some well known names. They must have the ability to contribute meaningfully to discussions and plans, and should also constitute those who are being sought for future full board membership.

An advisory board can be a powerful tool that expands the knowledge and public perception of the corporation without the cumbersomeness of creating a legal bureaucracy. The advisory board members can hold their positions for a limited time, allowing for the release of some advisory board members, or for retaining others. When choosing a board of directors always obtain a commitment and agreement to the mission statement before the appointment.

Always have a simple means of retiring a board member if they do not fit in.

Remember, a disgruntled board member who stays on can do untold damage to an organisation if a plan has not been put into place for swift, silent removal. It is easy to put people on a board . . . but often difficult to remove them!

A PREAMBLE FOR PRESENTATION

We are now getting ready to create a corporate mission statement that works, taking into consideration the ten points that we have just covered as the preparation for the task that lies ahead. I would counsel you at this stage to read again the principles of goal setting as provided for in the preparation of the personal mission statement, and urge you to accept the same goals formula for the creation of your own corporate goals.

I must repeat again that in the setting of corporate goals, as with all these principles, clear, close observation of the process, not the project, is of paramount importance. Whatever happens, do not muddy the waters by disagreeing with the project, as I am not expecting that you could or even should agree with it, because it is just a selection from a number of corporate goals and is probably not transferable to another corporation or organisation. Again I encourage you to follow the *process*, not the *project*, and if you need specific help on goal setting, obtain a copy of my book *How to Reach Your Life Goals*, or write a letter to the World Centre for Entrepreneurial Studies at the address shown at the beginning of this book. The difference with a corporate mission statement is threefold.

Notes

Firstly, it must be presented as a public and general mission statement for all who care to read it, which would include suppliers, customers and all those working for the corporation.

Secondly, there must be a fuller, more comprehensive working goals programme for those charged with the responsibility of ensuring its full implementation.

Thirdly, there needs to be a sloganising of the mission statement, either in part or in full, for inspiration, advertising and customer relations. The following are the eight steps to achievement, which are under the same headings as expressed in the personal mission statement, but distinctively different in their working out in the arena of corporate dynamics and achievement. The variation from a personal mission statement is that the eight steps are not in relationship to the title, and so number one becomes number two, which means that the vehicle pre-dates the goal. Some of the other steps in which a special emphasis fits better, have been changed, sometimes criss-crossing those which were demonstrated in different ways in the personal mission statement formula. Keep in mind at all times that although the mission statement contains a goal, it is not a goals programme and should only be used as the journey to fulfil the detailed goals programme. The other noticeable difference in the corporate mission statement is its length, which is somewhat shorter than the personal mission statement because the corporate mission statement always has the added advantage of a major goals plan to support it. Also, some areas of attention are not as easy to declare in short form. Now we will list very simply the eight steps to achievement in preparation for a corporate mission statement.

1. The vehicle

2. The goal

3. The commitment

4. The qualification

5. The positioning

6. The destination

7. The assessment

8. The creed

Notes

1. The Corporate Vehicle

In a corporate structure the vehicle or the product becomes the prominent item because all management, finance, marketing and production has its focus on this as the primary reason for being, and without the vehicle (product or service) then no corporate entity exists. With the selection of your vehicle, a great deal of consideration must be given to the limitations that are both inwardly and outwardly put upon it. For instance, if you are going to build a marketing corporation, some consideration needs to be given as to what limits you will put on it.

You may want to market kitchenware; but the decision needs to be made as to whether you are in the home kitchen supply business or the engineering and design business, understanding that the latter would provide more options as growth and opportunities present themselves.

If, for instance, you manufacture porcelain lavatory pans, are you going to restrict yourself to that or are you going to consider that you are in the bathroom accessory or the porcelain and glass moulding business? As an example, (remember, follow the process not the project) I would suggest that the exploration, the finding and the marketing of oil fuels could be our vehicle.

Now the question that must be answered here is — am I in the fuel business or the energy business? I am sure we all see ahead new types of fuels and energy units. Having decided that I am in the energy business, and that is my vehicle for my corporate mission statement, a sample corporation mission statement needs to be presented to cover all of these variables.

Corporate Vehicle — Suggested Mission Statement

The corporation has been established and will continue for the production and the marketing of energy.

2. The Corporate Goal

Once a vehicle has been established then a goal setting its time, size and variables must be established. The corporate goals programme must be set and agreed to by the leaders, and confirmed by the board of directors. To be useful it must be documented and detailed in short range, medium range and long range planning. This part of the corporate mission statement should not be a detailed goals programme, but it should present the direction.

Corporate Goal — Suggested Mission Statement

Our goal is to lead in the production of quality and diversified energy that will meet the market needs of a global economy.

Notes

3. The Corporate Commitment

The commitment to reach the corporate goal must be expressed in words that reflect a discipline of equal measure and it must be spelt out in terms that can be easily grasped by all. A very necessary part of the corporate mission statement is to have it so directionally worded that it can be used as a motivational tool throughout the entire corporation.

Corporate Commitment — Suggested Mission Statement

The commitment to satisfy our corporate goal will be reflected in our effort and purpose, and sustained by internal and external examination.

4. The Corporate Qualification

Reaching a corporate goal requires a mission that will have proven, capable people and attainments to match the needs at every level. This can be expressed as a focal point in the corporate mission statement. In effect, it means that those who are chosen as key players must have the proven quality to lead, and in turn select the quality methods to manage and the quality tools to work with. It means that not only must the management and field personnel have quality, but it needs to be demonstrated at every level. The qualification of personnel must continually be upgraded to position the corporation on the front line of new discoveries and techniques.

Corporate Qualification — Suggested Mission Statement

Our personnel, product and service will accept as qualification the results of the market place.

5. The Corporate Positioning

The most important step in positioning is to be at the crucial point of timing and location of opportunities.

The second step is to be as sure as you can that the perception of the advantage is equal to the fact. It is so important to have a plan to be involved in whatever is available that it will put you in the box seat to observe opportunities so that you can capitalise on them.

Get involved in the industry, science and government discussions that can help you keep in touch, while at the same time, conduct in-depth investigations that could prove profitable to your own corporation. To reduce all of this to a corporate mission statement is difficult, but not impossible, so let's try.

Notes

Corporate Positioning — Suggested Mission Statement

Our insightful projections and effective communication will provide many leadership advantages.

6. The Corporate Destination

The object of the corporate mission statement is to point clearly to the goal, which is the final destination. To reach the destination a sense of practical purpose and growth must be built into the corporate mission statement to allow all those involved to ask themselves the question, "Can I grow as the corporation grows?" The destination will, at times, change some of its features because of unpredictable developments that are bound to occur, but we must be prepared for this. Build into the mission statement room for growth and variables for people, products and services, so that you can adapt to the unexpected interruptions along the way.

Corporate Destination — Suggested Mission Statement

Understanding that progress ultimately brings change, we will refocus our corporate goals, thereby stimulating all who participate towards that target.

7. The Corporate Assessment

The assessment of any corporate goals is accomplishment and profit. They will always come in that order. Without wise planning and economic prudence, success in the corporate world is impossible. Accomplishment in the correct way is always followed by the appreciation of money, and if we have any doubts about that, all we need to do is ask at the highest or the lowest level of the workforce and the substance of that statement will soon be demonstrated.

Unless measurable assessment in terms of market advantage, production, services and financial expenditure and return are calculated for feedback and strategies, it would be like playing football without goal posts, scoreboards or a game plan. All of this can be strategically placed within the corporate mission statement.

Corporate Assessment — Suggested Mission Statement

The performance of our product, personnel and investment will be regularly assessed to correct inaccuracies.

Notes

8. The Corporate Creed

Every corporation needs to have a substantial statement of integrity that declares to all concerned the
morality that governs its actions. Although rarely used
or looked at in the past, the ethics of a corporation are
now being spotlighted by many of the regulatory auth-
orities and the public. An ethics or morality statement
from a corporation sets it apart and creates confidence
and commitment that can even supersede salaries and
opportunity.

Corporate Creed — Suggested Mission Statement

*All corporate activities will respect the ethics of
confidence, clarity and truth and depend upon all
those involved to respond with loyalty to the corporate
goals and mission.*

COMPLETED CORPORATE MISSION STATEMENT

This corporation has been established and will continue for the production and the marketing of energy.

Our goal is to lead in the production of quality and diversified energy that will meet the market needs of a global economy.

The commitment to satisfy our corporate goal will be reflected in our effort and purpose and sustained by internal and external examination.

Our personnel, product and service will accept as qualification the results of the market place.

Our insightful projections and effective communication will provide many leadership advantages.

Understanding that progress ultimately brings change, we will refocus our corporate goals, thereby stimulating all who participate towards that target.

The performance of our product, personnel and investment will be regularly assessed to correct inaccuracies.

All corporate activities will respect the ethics of confidence, clarity and truth and depend upon all those involved to respond with loyalty to the corporate goals and mission.

Assessing the Dynamics of Your Mission Statement

Let me suggest five easy ways to monitor and measure the continued effectiveness of your dynamic mission statement that works.

CHAPTER SEVEN

Assessing The Dynamics of Your Mission Statement

Monitoring the Mission

As you come towards the end of this book I hope you have grasped the principles I have shared and are now ready to put into action what you have learned. Now I suggest that you lock in some regular time to refresh yourself on each of the principles.

I am reminded so often of my own ineptness when something goes wrong with a piece of machinery or a special mixture I may use at our cattle farm. The first thing we do to correct the situation is to go back and read the instructions. Inevitably we find that we have overlooked something. So do what you do when painting your house — if the mixture doesn't do the job, go back and read the instructions on the label on the tin.

Now let me suggest five easy ways to monitor and measure the continued effectiveness of your dynamic mission statement that works.

1. Does everyone feel included?

Isolation for anyone who has a role to play in the working out of your mission will create blockages. For a personal goal, where family and friends are involved and needed, anyone who is diffident or unaware about the mission can cause it to flounder. In major corporations and even small businesses or projects, an understanding of a mission statement is essential and clarity of perception relating to facts needs to be assured.

2. Has it inspired a culture?

A corporation that tends to form its identity and character from the mission statement as it is expressed and demonstrated by the management sometimes receives crossed signals from senior management conflicting with the mission, which is sure death to any corporate culture. The tendency is to evaluate a personal mission statement in respect to a person's value system, or philosophy, which reflects in an ethical way the reality of their commitment.

3. Do outsiders clearly understand it?

The best way to monitor the mission statement is to listen to your customers, who will mirror the way they see the company they are dealing with. One friend of mine used to disguise his voice and phone his own company seeking service and understanding of the company's culture, which gave him a direct insight into how his mission was understood by his staff. An individual with a mission can be sure the descriptive responses from other people will provide a guide of the accepted level.

4. Have all the distinctives been covered?

Feedback by way of difficulties caused by omissions can readily identify distinctives that have been over-looked, both personally and corporately. Use caution, however, in making changes, especially to your dynamic mission statement that works, because if it is not a long term distinctive that needs to be inserted, then you may create more confusion than confidence.

Notes

Test and try alterations and only after absolute assessment should you make any change. If you change a number of times, you are suggesting that your mission is a vacillation programme rather than a confirming document.

5. What is its relationship with the productive output?

The title of this assessment principle seems somewhat superfluous because it describes what seems to be the obvious, but often the obvious can be obscured through argument or circumstances. Continually ask the question, "Is the mission relating to the reality of our productive output in measurable ways?" If not, first look at the adherence to the mission, then the vehicle and finally the goal.

As a final piece of advice that may be helpful, consider sloganising some parts of your mission statement in your discussions, correspondence, advertising and speeches to declare in certain terms the direction you are travelling.

For example, the corporate mission statement given in the previous chapter could have the slogan, "New Ways to New Energy for A New Millennium!"

In conclusion let me leave you with a little story. From time to time my grandchildren sit on my knee at our farm and ask me to tell them a story. As I start to move into the drama of this make-believe, thinking all the time of what I am going to say next as I make up some great adventure, occasionally I may stop to gather my thoughts and within a split second they call out in unison, "What then?" So I am stimulated continually throughout the story. "What then?" "What then?" My anxious audience waits breathlessly for the next action to unfold.

So, as a closing remark, let me ask you the question that they have so often posed to me, as you reach your final destination and seek the fulfilment of your goals: "What then?" "What then?" "What then?"

Bon voyage.

Notes

A Few Added Thoughts

If you are already a C.E.O. or a President of a corporation, I trust that the information that has been shared in this book will stimulate some fresh innovative thoughts about your own responsibilities. If you are an individual seeking to create a personal mission statement, then I trust that the corporate insight has been of some help to you as well.

I believe that this may be the first attempt in business literature to come to grips with the knotty ramifications of a mission statement and if you have anything to add to what I have already written, I would be pleased to hear from you.

Profiles

Peter J Daniels, President and Founder

World Centre for Entrepreneurial Studies

Peter J Daniels

President and Founder

WORLD CENTRE FOR ENTREPRENEURIAL STUDIES

He came from a disadvantaged background and his early years were plagued with illiteracy and ignorance; yet he built a large business in real estate and serves on international boards extending to the four corners of the earth.

For a third of a century he has successfully studied, absorbed and experienced first-hand, the elusive field of business and at times worked with some of the most dynamic corporate and intellectual giants of this century.

He has a no-debt philosophy, is personally wealthy and readily adjusts to any situation. His keen intellect, experience and sharp mind produces simple, effective answers to complex problems with a commitment to the free enterprise system within benevolent boundaries and under strong principles. He is an international author of substance and quantity and one of the world's highest paid public speakers.

His network of contacts throughout the world has come as a result of an involvement over a third of a century which incurs as many as two hundred air flights annually to meet schedules — but he is always contactable to meet any genuine professional need.

World Centre for
Entrepreneurial Studies

The World Centre for Entrepreneurial Studies is a high performance organisation seeking to anticipate corporate, government and individual requirements into the 21st century.

The uniqueness of this organisation is demonstrated by its aggressive approach in providing information and education relevant to the challenge and the location of the need.

Because of tradition, debt and fixed locations, normal universities and business schools find it increasingly difficult to meet the stringent demands of the ever-changing world markets and economies.

Not bound by any of these restraints, equipped with regular international reports, and with grass roots sensitivity, the World Centre for Entrepreneurial Studies responds to organisations and governments by travelling anywhere in the world to the point of need within the client's time-frame, presenting the information or challenge required with outstanding success.

Exclusive corporate and staff strategic planning, tutorials, and futuristic surveys, can be created to obtain competitive advantage and help predict new trends. Seminars and conferences by way of selected tutorial presentations, or complete conference agenda, confidential strategies and management can be provided to give an effective results boost to any industry.

Confidential counselling and consultancy can provide reassurance and direction, allowing decisions to be made with new and different insights and information.

The World Centre for Entrepreneurial Studies seminars are some of the largest and most effective in the world and the small group workshops provide a hands-on tutorial of exceptional standards.

All tutorial programmes, books, videos and manuals are exclusive and are soundly researched and performance based, covering subjects such as long term strategic planning, value systems, goal setting, crisis management, motivation, marketing, public speaking, time management, sales, financial independence, attitudes for success and how to develop your own personal destiny, and are readily available throughout the world.

The World Centre for Entrepreneurial Studies has become a world leader in the field of entrepreneurship because of one reason — "IT GETS RESULTS".

PHOENIX FIRST PASTORS COLLEGE
13613 N. Cave Creek Rd.
Phoenix, AZ 85022